MIND OVER MATTER

Breaking Free From Mental Confinement

Trévon Ricks

INTRODUCTION

Have you ever felt trapped by your own thoughts, as if your mind is a locked cell, holding you back from your true potential? You're not alone. Many of us live within the invisible walls we've built over time—walls made of fear, self-doubt, and limiting beliefs.

These mental prisons can be just as confining as any physical barrier, keeping us from pursuing our dreams, embracing our true selves, and living the life we deserve. But what if I told you that the key to breaking free from this mental confinement lies within your grasp? Imagine a life where your thoughts empower rather than imprison you, where you can dismantle the chains of negativity and step into a world of boundless possibilities. This isn't just a lofty idea; it's a reality you can achieve. In "Mind Over Matter: How to Break Free from Mental Confinement," we'll embark on a journey to unlock the doors of your mind and release the incredible power within. This book will equip you with the tools to identify the thoughts that keep you stuck, rewrite the stories that limit you, and cultivate the resilience to push past any barrier. Get ready to transform your mind from a place of confinement into a space of freedom, creativity, and limitless potential. It's time to escape the prison of your mind and step into the life you were meant to live.

TABLE OF

CONTENTS

CHAPTER 1

UNDERSTANDING THE PRISON OF THE MIND

The prison of the mind isn't built overnight. It's constructed over years, often without us even realizing it. Imagine for a moment a young child, full of curiosity and wonder, believing they can be anything they want. There's no fear of failure, no self-doubt, just pure potential. But as that child grows, they begin to encounter limitations—sometimes imposed by others, sometimes self- imposed. "You're not good enough." "You'll never succeed at that." "People like us don't do things like that." Each time they hear these words, a brick is added to the wall, and slowly but surely, the minds' prison starts to take shape. Before we go any further, let's be clear about one thing: this mental prison is entirely self-made. That doesn't mean you're to blame for it—society, family, friends, and life experiences all play their part—but it does mean you have the power to dismantle it.

The first step to breaking free is understanding how it was built in the first place.

The Bricks of Limiting Beliefs

Limiting beliefs are the bricks that form the walls of your mental prison. These are the deeply held convictions that restrict your actions and thoughts. They might be about what you think you're capable of, how you see the world, or what you believe is possible for you. Often, these beliefs are formed in childhood, influenced by parents, teachers, and early life experiences. For example, if you were told repeatedly that you weren't good at math, you might have built a belief that you're just not a "math person." That belief, once established, becomes a self-fulfilling prophecy—

you avoid math, struggle with it when you can't avoid it, and confirm to yourself over and over again that you're bad at it. But here's the facts: these beliefs aren't necessarily true. They're just thoughts that have been repeated often enough to become ingrained in your mind. And just as they were created, they can be deconstructed. The Bars of Fear and Self-Doubt, If limiting beliefs are the bricks, fear and self-doubt are the bars that keep you locked in.

Fear of failure, fear of judgment, fear of the unknown—these are all powerful forces that can paralyze you, preventing you from taking action. Self-doubt, on the other hand, is that nagging voice in the back of your mind that questions your every move: "What if I'm not good enough? What if I fail? What will people think?" The thing about fear and self-doubt is that they feed off each other. The more you doubt yourself, the more afraid you become, and the more afraid you are, the more you doubt your abilities. It's a vicious cycle, and it can keep you locked in your mental prison indefinitely if you let it.

The Invisible Chains of Routine and Comfort Routines

can be a good thing—they provide structure and predictability in our lives. But when they become too rigid, they can also turn into chains that keep us stuck in place. Comfort, too, can be deceptive. It feels good to stay in your comfort zone, but it also keeps you from growing and evolving. The key is to recognize when your routines and comfort zones are no longer serving you. If you find yourself doing the same things day in and day out without any real sense of progress, it's time to break free.

The walls of your mental prison may be built of limiting beliefs, but the chains that keep you there are often your own unwillingness to step into the unknown. To break free, understanding the prison of the mind is the first step to freedom. It's about recognizing the limiting beliefs, fears, and routines that have kept you confined. But understanding is only the beginning. The real work comes in dismantling those walls and breaking those chains, one brick, one bar, one link at a time. In the chapters that follow, we'll dive deeper into how to identify and challenge these mental barriers. You'll learn practical techniques for rewriting your inner narrative, overcoming fear, and stepping out of your comfort zone. It's time to unlock your mind and discover the freedom that awaits beyond the walls you've built.

CHAPTER 2

IDENTIFY YOUR MENTAL CHAINS

Recognizing that you're in a mental prison is one thing; identifying the specific chains that hold you there is another. These chains—limiting beliefs, fears, and self- doubts—are often so ingrained in our thinking that they feel like an inseparable part of who we are. But let me tell you from personal experience: they're not. I spent years behind bars—both physically and mentally—and I can assure you that the mental chains were just as confining as the physical ones, if not more so. But once I learned to identify those chains, I began the journey to breaking free, and now, I want to help you do the same.

The Weight of Limiting Beliefs

When I was serving time, I initially saw it as time wasted— years of my life that I could never get back. I was consumed by regret and anger, feeling like my potential had been snuffed out. But as the days turned into weeks and then months, I started to realize something: this time wasn't wasted unless I allowed it to be. In fact, this was time I needed—time to reflect on my life, my choices, and most importantly, the beliefs that had led me to this point.

One of the biggest revelations was recognizing the limiting beliefs I had carried with me for so long. For example, I used to believe that because of my past, my options for the future were limited. That belief weighed on me heavily, influencing every decision I made—or didn't make. This is a common mental chain. We often believe that our past defines us, that our mistakes are permanent markers of our worth or potential. But here's the truth: your past is only one chapter in your story, not the entire book. Recognizing this was a turning point for me. I realized that I didn't have to be defined by my mistakes, and that belief alone started to loosen the chains that had held me back for so long.

The Fear of Failure and Judgment

Another chain that kept me locked in was the fear of failure and judgment. After being released, I wanted to rebuild my life, but the fear of failing was often in my subconscious.

What if I tried to start a business and it didn't work out? What if people judged me for my past? These questions would pop up in my mind, but I never allowed these thoughts to keep me from taking any meaningful steps forward.

Then I realized something: the fear of failure is often worse than the failure itself. And the truth is, people will always have opinions, but those opinions don't define who you are or what you're capable of. I had to confront this fear head-on. I started small—making plans, setting goals, and taking those first tentative steps. The more I acted, the more I realized that failure isn't something to be feared; it's a necessary part of growth. And judgment? It's just noise that fades into the background when you're focused on your purpose.

Breaking the Chains of Comfort

was another chain I had to break. After years of incarceration, routine became a safety net. It was easy to fall into predictable patterns, even when they weren't serving me. But comfort can be deceiving. It lulls you into a false sense of security, keeping you from stepping out and trying something new. For me, it was comfortable to stick with what I knew, even if what I knew wasn't leading me anywhere.

Breaking out of that comfort zone was crucial. I had to push myself to take risks, to challenge myself, and to be okay with the discomfort that comes with growth.

The Pressure of Expectations

One of the most challenging chains I had to face was the pressure of expectations, particularly those of my mother. I had already put her through so much with my past choices, and the thought of disappointing her again weighed heavily on me. I wanted to make her proud, to show her that I had turned my life around. But this pressure also brought its own fears—the fear of failing in her eyes, of not being able to live up to the expectations I had set for myself. This is where belief in yourself becomes crucial. It's easy to let the fears and doubts of others seep into your mind, especially when you don't want to let down those you care about. But at some point, you have to realize that their fears don't define your capabilities. I knew I couldn't let the fear of failure—or the fear of disappointing my mother—paralyze me. I had to take the necessary risks to succeed, even if it meant stepping out into the unknown.

What beliefs do you hold about yourself that limit your potential? What fears keep you from taking the next step? What comfort zones are you stuck in? These are the questions you need to ask yourself. For me, it was about recognizing that my past didn't define me, that failure wasn't something to fear, and that comfort could be a trap. Once I identified those chains, I could start breaking them, one by one. In this chapter, I've shared a bit of my journey to help you see that you're not alone in this. We all have mental chains, but we also all have the power to break free from them. The next step is learning how to dismantle those chains, and in the following chapters, we'll explore the tools and strategies you can use to do just that. Remember, the prison of your mind is one you have the power to escape—starting right now.

CHAPTER 3

THE POWER OF SELF- AWARENESS

Self-awareness is the foundation upon which all personal and professional growth is built. It's the ability to look inward, recognize your thoughts, emotions, and behaviors, and understand how they shape your life. Without self- awareness, you're navigating life on autopilot, reacting to external situations without understanding why you do what you do. Once you unlock the power of self-awareness, you begin to control your responses to the world around you, instead of being controlled by it. At its core, self- awareness helps you identify your strengths and weaknesses. Understanding where you excel and where you need improvement is crucial for growth. Whether you're starting a business, pursuing a new career, or working on personal relationships, knowing who you are and how you operate makes all the difference. If you are unaware of your weaknesses, you are likely to keep making the same mistakes, wondering why you can't seem to break through certain barriers.

On the flip side, recognizing your strengths allows you to leverage them to your advantage, pushing you toward success with intention and purpose. When you are self-aware, you stop blaming external circumstances for your failures. Instead, you take full accountability for your actions and outcomes. This mindset shift is crucial. It allows you to see challenges as opportunities for growth rather than obstacles. For example, if you're struggling with your finances, a lack of self-awareness may lead you to believe that it's because of external factors—like the economy or bad luck. But if you're aware of your spending habits, your attitudes toward money, and your past decisions, you'll be able to identify exactly what needs to change. From there, you can develop a plan and take action to improve your situation. Self- awareness also plays a huge role in emotional intelligence. It helps you recognize your triggers, the things that set you off, and how you react in stressful situations. When you understand your emotions and why you feel the way you do, you can regulate those emotions more effectively. For entrepreneurs or anyone in a leadership role, this is a game-changer.

When you're self-aware, you're not easily swayed by emotions like frustration or anger. Instead, you make decisions based on logic, insight, and long-term vision, which leads to more consistent and level-headed leadership. Another critical aspect of self-awareness is understanding how you come across to others. It's not just about what you intend to communicate, but how your words, actions, and energy are perceived. If you're unaware of the impact you have on others, you may unintentionally damage relationships or miss opportunities to connect. Whether you're leading a team or working with clients, self-awareness allows you to communicate more effectively, collaborate more smoothly, and build stronger, more trusting relationships. Ultimately, self- awareness is about gaining clarity. Clarity about who you are, what you want, and how to get there. Without it, you're just moving through life blindly. But with it, you're empowered to make better decisions, live with purpose, and create the life you truly desire. Self-awareness isn't just a tool for success—it's the key to unlocking your full potential.

Self-awareness forces you to confront uncomfortable truths about yourself, but it's in that discomfort that real transformation happens. When you truly understand yourself—your motives, fears, and habits—you can start to question the story you've been telling yourself. Are you living by beliefs that limit you? Are you holding onto identities that no longer serve you? Self-awareness challenges you to break free from the labels and constraints that have kept you stuck, allowing you to become the person you were meant to be. Many people go through life without questioning the narrative running in their minds. They think they're not good enough, not smart enough, or not worthy of success. But self-awareness opens the door to rewriting those narratives. You start to recognize that these limiting beliefs are just stories you've accepted as truth. When you become aware of them, you gain the power to change them. That's where the real transformation begins—not in trying to be someone you're not, but in becoming fully aware of who you already are and realizing the potential that lies within.

Self-awareness isn't a one-time revelation. It's an ongoing process of discovery, growth, and realignment. And once you've begun that journey, you'll find that the next step naturally leads to reshaping the way you see yourself and the world around you. In the next chapter, we'll dive deeper into how to rewrite your inner narrative, exploring how the stories we tell ourselves shape our reality—and how we can take control of that story to create a life filled with purpose, power, and possibility.

True liberation starts with understanding yourself. When you know who you are, what drives you, and what holds you back, you can break the mental chains that have kept you confined and step into a life of limitless potential. Self-awareness gives you the power to reclaim your freedom. And once you've unlocked that, the world opens up in ways you never thought possible.

CHAPTER 4

REWRITING YOUR INNER NARRATIVE

Every one of us carries a story in our minds—a narrative we tell ourselves about who we are, what we're capable of, and what we deserve in life. The problem is, many of these stories are written for us, not by us. They're shaped by our environment, experiences, and the expectations others placed upon us. These narratives, often built on fear, past failures, or limiting beliefs, confine us mentally, keeping us from reaching our full potential. But the beauty of being human is that we have the power to rewrite our stories at any moment. You are not bound to the narrative that has dictated your past. You have the power to craft a new one, one that aligns with your vision, your purpose, and your highest potential. Rewriting your narrative begins with understanding that the story you've been living by is just that—a story. It's not set in stone, and it's certainly not an unchangeable truth. The first step in breaking free from mental confinement is recognizing that your beliefs about yourself have been shaped by experiences and perceptions, but they do not define you. Self-awareness, which we discussed in the last chapter, is the key to unlocking this realization.

Once you understand how you've been shaped by external factors, you can take the reins and start reshaping that narrative to serve you, rather than limit you. In my own journey, I had to confront the story I had been living by for years. After being released from federal prison, I realized the narrative that once defined me—one of mistakes, loss, and guilt—was not serving my future. I had to break down that old narrative and reconstruct a new one that reflected the man I wanted to become. I wasn't a failure; I was someone who had faced adversity and was determined to rise above it. I wasn't confined to my past; I was writing a future filled with purpose, financial freedom, and service to others. And I'm living proof that you can rewrite your own story, no matter how far off track you think you've gone. Here's how you can begin to rewrite your own narrative:

Identify the Limiting Beliefs

The first step is to get clear about the limiting beliefs that have been holding you back. Ask yourself: What have I been telling myself about who I am? What labels have I accepted that don't align with who I truly want to be? Perhaps you believe you're not worthy of success, or that because you've made mistakes in the past, you can't achieve greatness. These beliefs are chains, keeping you locked in a mental prison.

The only way to break free is to identify them and challenge their validity. Write them down. Then ask yourself, "Is this true, or is this just a story I've been telling myself?"

Challenge the Old Narrative

Once you've identified those limiting beliefs, it's time to challenge them. Remember, these are not facts; they're stories you've internalized based on your past experiences. Just because you believed something about yourself doesn't mean it's true. For example, if you've always believed you're bad with money because of past financial mistakes, challenge that narrative. Recognize that those mistakes don't define your financial future. You have the power to learn, grow, and rewrite your financial story. You have the ability to master money management and create wealth. The same applies to any area of your life where you've felt confined—relationships, career, or self-worth.

Create a New Story

Now that you've challenged the old narrative, it's time to create a new one. This new story should be rooted in the person you want to become, not the person you've been in the past. It should reflect your potential, your dreams, and your true self. Think of this new narrative as a blueprint for your life moving forward.

Instead of saying, "I'm not good enough," your new story might be, "I am capable of achieving anything I set my mind to." Instead of, "I always mess up," it's, "I learn from every experience and grow stronger." Write this new narrative down. Make it clear, positive, and aligned with your goals. This is the story that will guide you as you move forward.

Visualize Your New Narrative

Visualization is a powerful tool when it comes to rewriting your narrative. Take time each day to close your eyes and imagine yourself living out this new story. See yourself as the person you want to become, achieving your goals and overcoming challenges with ease. Visualizing your new narrative helps to rewire your brain, making it easier to believe in this new version of yourself. When you repeatedly visualize your success, your mind begins to accept it as reality, and you start taking actions that align with your new story.

Take Consistent Action

A new narrative is meaningless without action. You must back up your new story with consistent steps toward the life you want.

This is where most people get stuck—they rewrite the narrative in their mind but fail to act on it. Don't let that be you.

If your new story is about becoming a successful entrepreneur, what steps can you take today to move closer to that goal? If your new narrative is about mastering your health, what daily habits can you implement to reflect that? Consistent action is what solidifies your new narrative and makes it your reality.

Reinforce Your New Story Daily

Rewriting your narrative isn't a one-time event. It's a daily practice of reinforcing your new beliefs and challenging any old thoughts that try to creep back in. Surround yourself with people, environments, and resources that support your new story. If old habits or doubts resurface, remind yourself of the new path you're on and the person you're becoming. This reinforcement is what keeps you on track and helps you fully embody your new narrative. In my own life, rewriting my narrative meant not allowing my past to dictate my future. I knew that to create the life I envisioned—one of financial freedom, spiritual growth, and helping others succeed—I had to let go of the old story that said I couldn't. My new narrative became one of empowerment, resilience, and purpose. And through consistent action, I began to see that new story come to life. It wasn't easy, but it was worth every moment of effort.

Conclusion:

Rewriting Your Narrative Is the Path to Freedom Rewriting your narrative is the ultimate act of mental freedom. It gives you the power to decide who you are, how you will live, and what you will achieve. You no longer have to be confined by old beliefs or past mistakes. You can choose a new path at any time, but it starts with understanding that you are the author of your own story.

The moment you take responsibility for that, the chains of mental confinement begin to fall away, and you can step into a life of true freedom and potential. In the next chapter, we'll dive into two of the biggest obstacles that hold us back from rewriting our narrative—**fear and self-doubt**. These mental barriers often keep us from taking the actions necessary to transform our lives. But once we learn how to confront and overcome them, nothing can stop us from living out our new, empowered stories.

CHAPTER 5

OVERCOMING FEAR AND SELF- DOUBT

Fear and self-doubt are two of the most powerful forces that can hold you back from achieving your dreams. They are the mental chains that keep you from taking risks, stepping into new opportunities, or pursuing the life you truly desire.

Overcoming fear and self-doubt isn't just about eliminating them—they're natural human emotions. It's about learning to manage and rise above them, turning what once held you back into fuel for your growth. In this chapter, we'll explore how to face fear and self-doubt head-on and overcome them step by step. We'll cover practical tools and strategies to help you break through these barriers and empower you to pursue your goals with confidence. But before we get into the steps, I want to take you back to my personal journey. After being released from prison, I wasn't filled with self-doubt, but I did feel as if the time that had passed while I was incarcerated had put me at a disadvantage. There were years I couldn't get back, years when I could've been building my career, my connections, and my future. I had to shift my perspective to see this time not as something that hindered me but as an experience that could benefit me.

I knew I couldn't change the past, but I could control what I did moving forward. I made the decision not to dwell on what I couldn't change but to focus on the time I had now—the opportunities in front of me—and make the most of them. It wasn't easy, but that shift in perspective was critical. It showed me that fear and doubt only have power when you give it to them. It's what you choose to focus on that matters. And just like I learned to focus on the present and the things I could control, you too can reframe your fears and doubts into tools for growth. Here's how.

Step 1: Recognize Fear and Self-Doubt as Normal

The first step in overcoming fear and self-doubt is recognizing that they are completely normal. Every person, no matter how successful or confident they seem, experiences fear and self-doubt at some point. These emotions are part of the human experience, and they don't mean you're weak or incapable. In fact, fear is often a sign that you're stepping outside of your comfort zone, which is where real growth happens. Acknowledge these feelings when they come up, but don't let them define you.

Step 2: Identify the Source of Your Fear

Fear and self-doubt don't appear out of nowhere—they have roots. To overcome them, you need to identify where they come from.

Ask yourself: What am I really afraid of? Am I afraid of failing? Am I afraid of what others will think? Am I afraid of success and the responsibilities that come with it? Once you identify the root cause, it becomes easier to address and overcome it. In my case, it wasn't fear of failure that held me back, but a fear of wasted time. I feared that too much time had slipped through my hands, that I was too late to make an impact. But once I identified that fear, I shifted my mindset and saw that I could still make the most of the time I had now. By identifying the root of your fear, you can challenge and shift it.

Step 3: Challenge the Narrative

Fear and self-doubt are often fueled by the stories we tell ourselves. We create worst-case scenarios in our minds and let them dictate our actions. But here's the truth: most of the things you fear will never happen. The stories you tell yourself are just that—stories. They aren't facts. Once you recognize that, you can challenge them. Ask yourself: What evidence do I have that this fear is valid? Have I failed before? If so, did I survive and learn from it? What's the worst thing that could happen if I try and fail? When you start to break down these stories, you realize that fear and self-doubt are built on shaky foundations.

Step 4: Take Small, Courageous Actions

Overcoming fear and self-doubt isn't about making one giant leap —it's about taking small, courageous actions that gradually build your confidence. Start by identifying one small step you can take today to move in the direction of your goals. It could be sending an email, making a phone call, signing up for a class, or even just writing down your goals. Every time you take action, no matter how small, you weaken the grip of fear and self-doubt. When I was starting my business, I had doubts about whether I could succeed. But instead of letting that stop me, I took small steps. I researched, networked, and learned everything I could about my industry.

Each action, no matter how minor it seemed, built my confidence and moved me closer to my goal.

Step 5: Visualize Your Success

One of the most powerful tools in overcoming fear and self-doubt is visualization. Close your eyes and imagine yourself succeeding. Picture yourself achieving your goals, overcoming obstacles, and standing in the place you want to be. The mind is a powerful tool, and when you visualize your success, you start to believe it's possible. This belief is the antidote to fear and self-doubt. The more you practice visualizing your success, the more your mind accepts it as a reality.

Step 6: Reframe Failure

One of the biggest reasons people don't take action is the fear of failure. But failure isn't something to fear—it's something to embrace. Every successful person has failed, often many times, before they reached their goals. Failure is not the end; it's part of the journey. When you reframe failure as a learning opportunity, it loses its power to paralyze you. Each failure is a lesson, a stepping stone toward success. The only real failure is in not trying. When I failed in the past, I used to see it as a confirmation that I wasn't good enough. But over time, I learned that failure was my greatest teacher. It showed me what didn't work and forced me to find new solutions. Embrace failure as a part of your process, and you'll find that fear loses its grip.

Step 7: Surround Yourself with Support

Fear and self-doubt thrive in isolation. When you're alone with your thoughts, it's easy to get caught in a spiral of negative thinking. That's why it's so important to surround yourself with people who believe in you, encourage you, and hold you accountable. Find a mentor, a support group, or even just a friend who can remind you of your potential when fear and doubt start to creep in. Surround yourself with people who uplift you, and you'll find it easier to rise above your fears.

Step 8: Commit to Growth

Overcoming fear and self-doubt isn't a one-time event—it's an ongoing process. As you grow and take on new challenges, fear and doubt will resurface in different forms. The key is to commit to continuous growth. Every time you face fear, you become stronger. Every time you push through self-doubt, you build confidence. Keep learning, keep taking action, and keep challenging yourself. Growth is a lifelong journey, and as long as you stay committed, fear and self-doubt will never control you.

Conclusion:

Fear and self-doubt don't have to be your enemies. In fact, they can be your greatest allies if you learn to face them head-on. They show you where you need to grow, where you need to take action, and where you need to challenge yourself. When you recognize fear and self-doubt for what they are—just emotions—you take away their power. As we move into the next chapter, we'll explore how to build unstoppable momentum in your life. Once you've learned to manage fear and self-doubt, the next step is learning how to create lasting change and keep pushing forward, no matter what challenges come your way.

CHAPTER 6

HARNESSING THE POWER OF VISUALIZATION

Visualization is one of the most potent tools for creating the life you desire. By vividly imagining your goals and dreams, you plant the seeds of possibility in your mind and set into motion a process that aligns your thoughts, emotions, and actions with achieving them. This chapter explores how to effectively harness the power of visualization to transform your reality.

The Science Behind Visualization

Visualization is not merely wishful thinking; it is a practice grounded in science. Studies have shown that mental imagery activates the same neural pathways as actual physical activity. When you visualize a goal, your brain rehearses the experience, strengthening the connections that will help you achieve it.

For instance, athletes often use visualization techniques to improve their performance. A basketball player might mentally rehearse sinking free throws, imagining the ball leaving their hands, arcing perfectly, and swishing through the net. This mental practice primes the brain and body to perform the task successfully when the time comes.

Similarly, you can use visualization to rehearse your goals, whether it's landing your dream job, improving your relationships, or building a thriving business. By consistently imagining yourself succeeding, you condition your mind to believe in your ability to achieve it.

A Personal Journey of Visualization

When I was incarcerated, visualization became a lifeline for me. I spent countless hours picturing myself in the position I wanted to be in, rather than focusing on my current circumstances. I imagined walking out of prison, building a successful career, and living the life I had always dreamed of. These vivid mental pictures helped me maintain hope and resilience, even on the toughest days.

This practice didn't just keep my spirits up—it gave me direction. By visualizing my goals, I was able to identify the steps I needed to take to make them a reality. It was as if I was rehearsing my future, programming my mind to seek out opportunities and stay committed to my vision. Visualization transformed my mindset and laid the foundation for the life I'm building today.

Be Clear and Specific

Begin by defining what you want in detail. Vague goals yield vague results. Instead of saying, "I want to be successful," envision what success looks like for you. Is it owning your own business? Living in a specific home? Spending more time with family? The clearer your vision, the more powerful the visualization.

Engage All Your Senses

To make your visualization as vivid as possible, engage all five senses. If your goal is to buy your dream car, imagine the way it looks, the feel of the steering wheel, the sound of the engine, the smell of the interior, and even the taste of celebration as you drive it off the lot.

Feel the Emotions

Emotions amplify the power of visualization. As you imagine your desired outcome, tap into the feelings you would experience if it were already a reality. Would you feel joy?

Gratitude? Excitement? Let those emotions wash over you as you visualize.

Practice Regularly

Consistency is key. Dedicate time each day to visualization, whether it's first thing in the morning, during a break, or before bed. Even five to ten minutes of focused visualization can yield remarkable results over time.

Take Inspired Action

Visualization alone is not enough. It must be paired with action. Use your mental imagery as a guide to take steps toward your goals. Each action, no matter how small, brings you closer to turning your vision into reality.

Overcoming Common Challenges

Some people struggle with visualization, thinking they're "not good at imagining things." If that's you, start simple. Use a photo or object that represents your goal as a focal point. For example, if you dream of traveling, look at pictures of your desired destination and imagine yourself there.

Another challenge is doubt. It's natural to feel skeptical, especially when your current reality feels far from your vision. Remember, visualization is not about ignoring your present circumstances; it's about believing in the possibility of change and using your imagination to fuel that belief.

Real-Life Applications

Here are a few practical ways to incorporate visualization into your daily life:

- Vision Boards: Create a collage of images and words that represent your goals. Place it where you'll see it often to keep your vision top of mind.

- Guided Visualization: Use audio recordings or apps that guide you through visualization exercises tailored to your goals.

- Journaling: Write down detailed descriptions of your desired outcomes as if they've already happened.

- Mind Movies: Create a short video with images and music that represent your goals and watch it regularly.

The Ripple Effect of Visualization

When you practice visualization consistently, you'll notice a ripple effect in your life. Your thoughts will become more aligned with your goals, your confidence will grow, and opportunities you hadn't noticed before will begin to appear. This isn't magic—it's the power of focus and intention at work.

Visualization is not just about creating a better future; it's about becoming the person who can achieve that future. By seeing yourself as capable, deserving, and empowered, you align your energy with the life you want to create.

Take a moment now to close your eyes and visualize one of your biggest goals. Imagine it as vividly as you can. Feel the emotions, see the details, and trust that you're planting the seeds of your future. The journey to your dreams begins in your mind—and with consistent practice, it will unfold in your reality.

"Your imagination is your preview of life's coming attractions."

— Albert Einstein

CHAPTER 7

BUILDING MENTAL RESILIENCE

Mental resilience is the foundation of personal growth, success, and fulfillment. Life is filled with challenges, but your ability to navigate them without losing focus, confidence, or hope determines how far you can go. In this chapter, we'll explore what it takes to build unshakable mental resilience so you can face adversity, adapt to change, and emerge stronger every time.

Understanding Mental Resilience

At its core, mental resilience is your capacity to recover from setbacks, maintain a positive outlook, and keep moving forward despite obstacles. It's not about avoiding difficulties but about learning to thrive in their presence.

Think of mental resilience as a muscle. The more you work on it, the stronger it becomes. Challenges then transform from insurmountable problems into opportunities for growth.

Why Mental Resilience Matters

Without resilience, even minor setbacks can feel overwhelming. On the other hand, with a strong mental foundation, you're able to:

- **Handle Stress:** Resilience helps you manage stress effectively, preventing it from taking a toll on your mental and physical health.

- **Stay Focused:** Instead of being derailed by challenges, you can stay focused on your goals.

- **Adapt Quickly:** Life is unpredictable. Resilience gives you the flexibility to adjust and find solutions.

- **Maintain Optimism**: *A resilient mindset keeps hope alive, even in the toughest times.*

Practical Strategies to Build Mental Resilience

1. **Reframe Challenges as Opportunities**

Rather than seeing obstacles as roadblocks, view them as stepping stones for growth. Ask yourself, "What can I learn from this?" or "How can this make me stronger?" Shifting your perspective transforms struggles into valuable life lessons.

2. **Cultivate Self-Awareness**

Understanding your thoughts and emotions is key to resilience. Practice mindfulness to become aware of negative thought patterns and replace them with empowering ones. Journaling can also help you reflect on your feelings and track your growth.

3. **Develop a Growth Mindset**

A growth mindset is the belief that your abilities and intelligence can be developed through effort and learning. Embrace challenges, see failure as a stepping stone, and celebrate progress—no matter how small.

4. **Strengthen Your Support System**

Resilience doesn't mean facing everything alone. Surround yourself with positive influences who uplift and inspire you. Whether it's friends, family, mentors, or support groups, having a strong network can make all the difference.

5. **Practice Gratitude**

Gratitude shifts your focus from what's going wrong to what's going right. By acknowledging the good in your life, you train your mind to find positivity even in difficult situations. Start a gratitude journal or take a few moments each day to reflect on what you're thankful for.

6. **Take Care of Your Physical Health**

Your mind and body are deeply connected. Regular exercise, proper nutrition, and sufficient sleep boost your mood, energy, and overall resilience. A strong body supports a strong mind.

7. **Set Realistic Goals**

Break big challenges into manageable steps. Achieving small wins builds confidence and keeps you motivated to tackle larger obstacles. Remember, resilience is built one step at a time.

8. **Learn to Let Go**

Holding onto past mistakes, regrets, or disappointments drains your energy. Practice forgiveness—for yourself and others—and focus on what you can control in the present moment.

A Personal Story of Resilience

When I was incarcerated, I faced a level of adversity that could have easily broken me. There were days when the weight of my circumstances felt unbearable. But instead of letting it crush me, I chose to focus on the future I wanted to create. I made a decision to not just survive but thrive.

Every day, I practiced visualization, imagined the life I was building, and used the time to develop my mind and skills. When things felt overwhelming, I leaned on the support of my family and kept reminding myself of my purpose. That period of my life tested my mental resilience like nothing else, but it also showed me just how strong I could be.

Resilience isn't about having an easy path; it's about finding the strength to keep walking, even when the road is rough. If I could do it in those circumstances, so can you.

Resilience in Action: Daily Practices

To integrate resilience into your life, try these daily habits:

- **Start Your Day with Affirmations:** *Repeat positive statements like, "I am strong" or "I can handle whatever comes my way."*

- **Practice Stress Management:** *Incorporate breathing exercises, meditation, or yoga to calm your mind.*

- **Learn Something New:** *Challenging yourself with new skills builds confidence and adaptability.*

- **Reflect on Your Wins:** *Take a moment to celebrate small victories every day.*

- **Create Boundaries:** *Protect your energy by saying no to negativity or tasks that don't serve your goals.*

The Ripple Effect of Resilience

Building mental resilience doesn't just benefit you—it impacts everyone around you. When you become more adaptable, positive, and focused, you inspire others to do the same. You create a ripple effect of strength and hope that extends far beyond yourself.

Resilience is a skill you can develop, no matter where you are in life. With consistent practice, you'll not only overcome challenges but thrive in ways you never thought possible.

Remember, resilience isn't about being perfect or never struggling. It's about rising every time you fall, learning from the experience, and moving forward with greater determination. Start building your mental resilience today, and watch as it transforms not just your life, but the lives of those around you.

CHAPTER 8

CREATING A NEW REALITY

The life you live today is a reflection of your past thoughts, beliefs, and actions. If you want to change your life, you must first change your reality—and that begins with changing your mindset. This chapter will guide you through the process of creating a new reality, empowering you to step into the life you truly desire.

The Foundation of a New Reality

Creating a new reality starts with the understanding that you are the architect of your life. Every decision, thought, and belief contributes to the structure of your existence. By taking responsibility for your present circumstances, you reclaim the power to design your future.

The Power of Belief

Your beliefs shape your reality. If you believe you are limited, you will live a limited life. If you believe you are capable, you will pursue opportunities that align with that belief. The key to creating a new reality is to examine and reprogram the beliefs that no longer serve you.

The Ripple Effect of Resilience

Building mental resilience doesn't just benefit you—it impacts everyone around you. When you become more adaptable, positive, and focused, you inspire others to do the same. You create a ripple effect of strength and hope that extends far beyond yourself.

Resilience is a skill you can develop, no matter where you are in life. With consistent practice, you'll not only overcome challenges but thrive in ways you never thought possible.

Remember, resilience isn't about being perfect or never struggling. It's about rising every time you fall, learning from the experience, and moving forward with greater determination. Start building your mental resilience today, and watch as it transforms not just your life, but the lives of those around you.

Steps to Shift Your Beliefs:

1. **Identify Limiting Beliefs**: Reflect on areas where you feel stuck and ask, "What beliefs might be holding me back?" Write them down.

2. **Challenge Those Beliefs:** Question their validity. Are they based on facts, or are they assumptions? Replace them with empowering beliefs.

3. **Reinforce New Beliefs:** Use affirmations, visualization, and action to embed your new beliefs into your daily life.

Visualization and Intention

As discussed in earlier chapters, visualization is a powerful tool for shaping your reality. Combine it with clear intention—a focused desire backed by belief and action—to accelerate the manifestation of your goals.

A Visualization Exercise:

1. Close your eyes and take a few deep breaths.

2. Imagine yourself living your dream life in vivid detail. Where are you? What are you doing? How does it feel?

3. Hold that image in your mind for a few minutes, letting the emotions of gratitude and excitement wash over you.

4. Open your eyes and write down the vision you just experienced. Use it as a guide to take daily steps toward your goals.

Taking Aligned Action

Visualization and belief are essential, but action is what turns dreams into reality. The key is to take aligned action—steps that are in harmony with your goals and values.

How to Take Aligned Action:

- **Set Clear Goals:** Break your vision into specific, measurable objectives.
- **Create a Plan:** Outline the steps you need to take and prioritize them.
- **Start Small:** Focus on one action at a time to build momentum.
- **Stay Consistent:** Commit to daily actions that move you closer to your vision.

The Role of Gratitude

Gratitude is a transformative practice that shifts your focus from lack to abundance. By appreciating what you already have, you open yourself to receive even more. Gratitude also reinforces your belief in a positive reality.

Daily Gratitude Practice:

- Each morning, write down three things you are grateful for.
- At the end of the day, reflect on what went well and why.
- Express gratitude to others whenever possible.

A Personal Story of Transformation

When I was at one of the lowest points in my life, I realized that the only way forward was to create a new reality. I started by visualizing the life I wanted—freedom, success, and purpose. I wrote down my goals, challenged my limiting beliefs, and committed to daily actions that aligned with my vision.

The journey wasn't easy, but every step brought me closer to the life I imagined. Today, I am living proof that you can transform your reality by changing your mindset, focusing on your vision, and taking consistent, aligned action.

Overcoming Resistance

Change often brings resistance, whether from within yourself or from others. Here's how to overcome it:

- **Internal Resistance**: Address fear and self-doubt by reminding yourself of your "why" and celebrating small victories.

- **External Resistance**: Stay true to your vision, even if others don't understand it. Surround yourself with people who support your growth.

The Ripple Effect of Creating a New Reality

When you create a new reality for yourself, you inspire others to do the same. Your transformation becomes a beacon of hope, showing what's possible with the right mindset, belief, and action.

The power to create a new reality is within you. It starts with a decision to believe in your potential and take steps toward the life you desire. Remember, you don't have to wait for the perfect moment—the perfect moment is now. Start today, and watch as your new reality unfolds before your eyes.

"Cherish your visions and your dreams as they are the children of your soul, the blueprints of your ultimate achievements."

-Napoleon Hill

CHAPTER 9

MAINTAING MENTAL FREEDOM

Congratulations on reaching the final chapter. By now, you've learned how to harness visualization, build resilience, and create a new reality. But transformation doesn't stop here. True success comes not just from achieving freedom, but from maintaining it—and that begins with protecting your most valuable asset: **your mind.**

Mental freedom is the ability to think, believe, and act without being shackled by fear, doubt, or external negativity. It's a state of clarity and control where you dictate the course of your life, regardless of circumstances. In this final chapter, we'll explore how to maintain mental freedom and live a life of continual growth and empowerment.

The Foundation of Mental Freedom

Mental freedom starts with awareness. Recognize that your thoughts shape your reality and that you alone are responsible for them. Maintaining mental freedom requires daily practice and vigilance, as life's challenges can easily pull you off course if you're not prepared.

Practical Strategies to Protect Your Mental Freedom

1. Guard Your Mind Against Negativity

Not every thought, opinion, or piece of information deserves your attention. Be intentional about what you consume. Limit exposure to toxic environments, negative news, and people who drain your energy. Instead, surround yourself with positivity, inspiration, and individuals who uplift you.

2. Master the Art of Letting Go

Holding onto past regrets, grudges, or disappointments weighs down your mental freedom. Practice forgiveness—for yourself and others. Release what no longer serves you and focus on the present moment, where your power truly lies.

3. Cultivate Inner Peace

Mental freedom flourishes in a peaceful mind. Incorporate mindfulness practices such as meditation, deep breathing, or journaling to center yourself. These habits create a mental sanctuary where you can process emotions and refocus your energy.

4. Stay Committed to Growth

Freedom isn't static; it's a dynamic process that requires continual growth. Challenge yourself to learn new skills, explore new perspectives, and expand your comfort zone. Growth not only strengthens your mind but also deepens your sense of purpose.

5. Set Clear Boundaries

Protect your mental space by setting boundaries with people, technology, and distractions. Learn to say no to anything that conflicts with your values or drains your energy. Boundaries are an act of self-respect and a declaration of your commitment to mental freedom.

A Personal Story of Maintaining Mental Freedom

After overcoming significant challenges and transforming my life, I realized that maintaining mental freedom was just as important as achieving it. There were moments when self-doubt and external pressures crept back in, threatening to derail my progress.

But I made a choice—every day—to prioritize my mental well-being. I learned to silence the noise, focus on my vision, and protect my peace. By committing to daily practices like mindfulness, gratitude, and reflection, I fortified my mental freedom and stayed on the path to growth.

You, too, have the power to make this choice every day. Freedom is not a destination; it's a lifestyle.

The Ripple Effect of Mental Freedom

When you maintain mental freedom, you don't just transform your life—you become a source of inspiration for others. Your clarity, confidence, and peace create a ripple effect, empowering those around you to seek their own freedom. This collective transformation has the power to change communities, families, and even the world.

A Call to Action

As you close this book, I want to leave you with one final thought: The journey to mental freedom is ongoing, but every step you take brings you closer to the life you deserve. You have all the tools you need to succeed. Now, it's up to you to take action.

Start today. Commit to protecting your mind, pursuing your vision, and living a life of purpose. Remember, every small step counts. With consistency and belief, you will achieve more than you ever thought possible.

Your journey doesn't end here—it begins now. The next chapter of your life is unwritten, and you hold the pen. Write it boldly, live it fully, and inspire others to do the same.

Thank you for taking this journey with me. You are capable of incredible things, and I can't wait to see the reality you create. Go forward with strength, purpose, and the unshakable belief in your ability to maintain the freedom you've worked so hard to achieve.

"Your mind is your greatest ally or your biggest obstacle. The moment you master it, you master your life. True freedom begins within."

-Trévon Ricks

Dedication

**First off—without the Guidance,
Protection, and Grace of God
I honestly don't know where I would be today.
I am eternally grateful.**

*In loving memory of my grandmother, Mary Noble,
and my grandfather, Benjamin Spry—your love, wisdom, and strength
will forever live within me.*

*To my Mom, Angel—there are no words to fully express what you mean
to me. Your love, strength, and unwavering support have shaped me
into the man I am today. Without you, I wouldn't be here, and I
wouldn't be the person I've become.*

*To my Dad, Greg—in a world full of lies, you never sugarcoated
anything, and I will always respect that.*

*To my cousin Dominique, my Aunt Torie, my Aunt Carolyn, and all my
family who stood by me through it all—your love, encouragement, and
belief in me gave me the strength to keep going, even in my darkest
moments.*

And to the few true friends who never wavered when I needed them most— you may not know the depth of your impact, but I do.

I dedicate this to all of you. Your love, loyalty, and support carried me when I couldn't carry myself. This journey, this transformation, and this book are as much yours as they are mine.

About the Author

At my lowest point—confined to a small prison cell, serving a five-year federal sentence—I experienced the most profound transformation of my life. Stripped of all distractions, I was forced to face myself, my thoughts, and my reality. It was in that solitude that I realized a powerful truth: my perspective, not my circumstances, shaped my reality. That realization changed everything. I made a choice to rewire my mindset, to see challenges as opportunities, and to reclaim control over my life. Through relentless self-education, discipline, and introspection, I discovered the principles that allowed me to break free mentally long before I was released physically. I wrote Mind Over Matter to share these life-changing insights with you. My mission is to help others shift their mindset, break free from mental limitations, and create a reality of success, no matter where they are starting from. If I could do it in my darkest moments, so can you.